# FLASH FRAMES
## A NEW POP CULTURE

### EDITED BY LAURIE DOLPHIN AND STUART S. SHAPIRO

Watson-Guptill Publications

First published in 2002 by Watson-Guptill Publications
a division of VNU Business Media, Inc.
770 Broadway, New York, NY 10003
www.watsonguptill.com

Library of Congress Cataloging-in-Publication Data

Flash frames : a new pop culture / edited by Laurie Dolphin and Stuart S. Shapiro.
        p. cm.
Includes index.
  ISBN 0-8230-1837-7
1.  Computer animation. 2.  Flash (Computer file) 3.  Web sites—Design.  I. Dolphin, Laurie.
II. Shapiro, Stuart S., 1948-
  TR897.7 .F55 2002
  006.6'96--dc21

                                                                                    2001004757

The principal typeface used in the composition of this book was Base 12 Sans
Manufactured in Malaysia
First printing, 2002
1 2 3 4 5 6 7 8 9 / 09 08 07 06 05 04 03 02

Senior Editor: Alison Hagge
Production Manager: Hector Campbell
Cover and interior design: Laurie Dolphin Design: Laurie Dolphin and Yusuf Sayman

*Flash Frames* is an Authorscape book production

Acknowledgements:
Lourdes Alba, Alkan Akdamar, Phil Alexander, Ralph Bakshi, Philip Berber, Kami Broyles, Ken Bunt, Pete Caban, Amy Capen, HH Ceolo, Gill Champion, Tom Coleman, Jason Colton, Rick Cruz, Julie Du Brow, Alan Douglas, Artist Forum, Joe Freitas, Dulcie Fulton, Fatma Arda Sayman, Eric Gardner, Claire Giard, Danny Goldberg, Roger Grod, Samuel Hadida, Sebastian Hassinger, Elaine and Harvey Herman, Ryan Honey, Hugo Kalf, Richard Kaufman, Josh Kimberg, Ayca Koseogullari, Barbara Krammer, Sven and Claire Krong from Click Media, Dave Lander, Michael and Tamara Lang, Walter Leaphart, Regina Livesay, Michel Madie, John McDermott, Susan McEowen, Steve Menkin, Lars Murray, Elaine O'Grady, Eric Oldrin, Heather Paster and Brett Fain, Harriet Pierce, Stephen Reid, Nina Resnick, Michael Roberson, Peter Rosenthal, Kao Rosman, Todd Rundgren, Bill Sager, our lovecats Jacqueline and Tim Sanders, Marc Scarpa, Mark Schneider, Adam Speilberger, Kevin Stein, Three, Mike Tunistra, Tal Vigderson, Kevin Walsh, Jamie Wilkinson, Dave Wise, and Eric Zimmerman. The Dolphin clan: Ben, Brian, Kathy, and Miles, as well as Bart, Pat, Murray, and Rita Stichman. The Shapiro clan: Burt, Ed, Dorian, Selma, Stella, and Jim Silberman. A special thanks to our agent, Deborah Warren Alexander, and to our most diligent editor, Alison Hagge.

And special Web site thanks to Ronen and Daniel of Magritte's Cow for designing and maintaining www.flashframes.org.

getting loaded . . .

> Flash Frames are those single frames of expression that flash across our visual landscape.

> In television production the term "flash frame" refers to a mistake—a single frame that does not belong in an editing sequence. These isolated frames usually flash by the naked eye at thirty frames per second without being consciously recognized. When MTV and music videos arrived on the scene twenty years ago many editing conventions were discarded. Nonlinear storytelling no longer followed traditional rules. At this point flash frames were embraced to create an effect, sometimes jarring. However, frames from music videos that filled a three-minute time zone with thousands of convergent images were all too weak to live on their own. The medium was not a singular, focused palette, but an impression of movement and sound that relied on a total, oversensory environment to achieve the action.

> The Internet and the dynamic and ubiquitous software program Flash have changed that creative landscape. Due to bandwidth considerations, videos and animations on the Internet are delivered at considerably slower frame rates than they are on broadband television. The process of developing Flash animation forces artists to create one image and frame at a time to build the moving picture. Similar to traditional animation, this technique demands that each frame is artistically complete. As a result Flash frames are now carefully orchestrated images that are rich in design and color. They have become individual works of art.

> Marcel Camus believed that a single frame of any film would and should define the film. A unique fingerprint, voiceprint, or DNA code identifies the individual. Likewise, the single frame of Flash art characterizes the larger work. In our world—which merges art, culture, and the reflection of history—these frames of creativity demonstrate the emergence of a new and interactive culture. One that exults freedom of expression without limitations. One where rules are set only to be broken. One where youth has no age.

> We live in a convergent, runaway pop culture where emerging art forms influence the mainstream. Flash art and animation on the Internet is the heartbeat of a new generation. This new technology—Flash—has fueled the independent artistic obsession to create and exhibit to the world at large. The open media delivery system of the Web enables the entire world Internet population to entertain and exhibit without restrictions.

> In a world where unreal, yet believable, images rule pop culture, the ability to tell a story and aggregate a communal experience through multiple levels of interactive texture will become more reliant on a single-frame art metaphor. Flash art will prove to define a new generation of media artists whose work will be able to be recognized by a single frame of their Flash art animation. The color saturation and digital ability to blow up, project, and print in high resolution will also enhance the spread of its influence to the point where feature films and mainstream television commercials will be created entirely in Flash.

> I've been lucky to have been there more than once, and it is always fun to be able to document the roots of any new creative cultural vein, particularly when it is so mercurial. The underbelly of the Internet pop culture will exhibit itself unabashed for years to come. These bands of creative artists and flashers are the founding fathers of their own truly independent inner artistic culture, which is expressed in a new art form with influences from all over the world.

> Flash—like jazz, rock 'n' roll, and hip-hop—is a new beat for a new generation.

> stuart s. shapiro

> Flash has been a boon to the animation community. It has enabled us to put a form of animation on our Web sites that we otherwise would not have been able to do, because of problems with bandwidths and everything. Flash allows us to create some very useable and detractive animation. Plus it makes those animations practical, available, and accessible to most people who own a computer.

> Flash is different from past animation. It is more basic, and a bit simpler. With regular animation you have more freedom. With Flash you are limited in the amount of drawing you can do, the amount of dialog you can have, and the amount of sound and music you can feature. In these ways doing animation for the Web limits you very much. However, using Flash enables you to work within those limits and turn out a very good product.

> Certainly anything that has its own look can be considered an art form. Flash has its own look, mainly because of its limitations. You can usually recognize animation that has been made with Flash. So it definitely is an art form. I do not know how permanent it is going to be, because the technology is bound to keep improving and changing. And as the technology improves, artists will be able to make animations for the Web that will be as good as the animations you can see on television or even in theaters.

> The Internet has allowed people to become animators who normally could not get into this business. Some artists are making animations for their Web sites that are positively brilliant. And these might be people who could never have gotten a job at an animation studio. So, what has happened is the Web has really made animators and entertainers of all types out of more people than would normally have ever entered those fields to become animators or entertainers. Now somebody who has something to say—whether it is in an art form with words, pictures, photos, or whatever—can get the message, whatever that might be, in front of the public by having his or her own Web site. In the past a person who had something that he or she wanted the world to know was often very frustrated—unless, of course, he or she was granted that one chance in a million to get a publisher or a producer to support his or her project.

> If you really have something you think is good, you can put it on your Web site. Then you can target certain people and say, "Hey, I want you to look at this. I think you will like it." Flash enables us to do this. It is a way to show animated versions of what your message is, in a condensed way, which hopefully will attract people.

> The minute computers evolved into a widespread method of communication and entertainment, I realized that this was the coming thing. And when the Web came along, you did not have to be a genius to realize that it was going to be the most powerful medium of communication that the world has ever known, because a) it is worldwide, b) it is instantaneous, and c) it is available and accessible to everybody. I had no idea that I might be an integral part of it, but I certainly knew that it was going to be the biggest thing of all.

> I do not think anybody is enough of a prophet to see the future of animation and Flash. The position that we are in now is really like having been at the very beginning of television, where someone showed a little screen and said, "Look, I can put a picture on this." I think the Internet has such possibility, and such potentiality, that if we were able to look twenty years ahead, we would not believe how all encompassing it is. I think the Internet will be part of every bit of our lives— our shopping, our entertainment, our finances, our education. Anything you can think of. I think that the Internet is going to be an octopus's tentacles, and is going to reach into every aspect of human endeavor.

> It is a funny thing. I am not a guy who looks back. I very rarely look back at things that I have written, or things that I have drawn of my properties, in the past. I seem to spend all of my time thinking of what I will do today, and what I am going to do tomorrow. And I think that twenty years from now, if I am around, which I think is unlikely, and I look back at what I have done up until now, I would probably say,. "God, that is so primitive. If only I could do it over and use all the technique and technical help that I have today, I could make it so much better."

> Every time I look at a comic book that I did years ago, I think, "I wish I could do that over again." I have always felt, and probably erroneously, that I am better today than I was yesterday. And, I always feel that whatever I did before, if I were doing it now—with hindsight, and because of experience—I could do it better.

> I think any artist needs just two things—dedication and practice. To be an artist, you have to draw, draw, draw, and never stop. Most artists start out by copying other artists, copying certain styles that they like, but at some point you have to get away from that and develop your own style. The ones who really make it big—whether they are actors or artists or writers—are the people who have their own immutable style. The other advice I would give is do not get discouraged. If you like what you are doing and you think it is good, but other people say it is not good, there is just as much of a chance that they are wrong, than that they are right. So many great artists and great writers have a history of rejection, before they have been discouraged. So you have to follow your own inclinations. And if you have the stuff, it will eventually show through. Do not let people say to you "that is not good" because it has not been done before or it is not the way they are doing it. There is a very good chance that if you are doing something that has not been done before, and it is not the way it is done now, you may be starting something new, a new style. You may be starting something great.

> stan lee

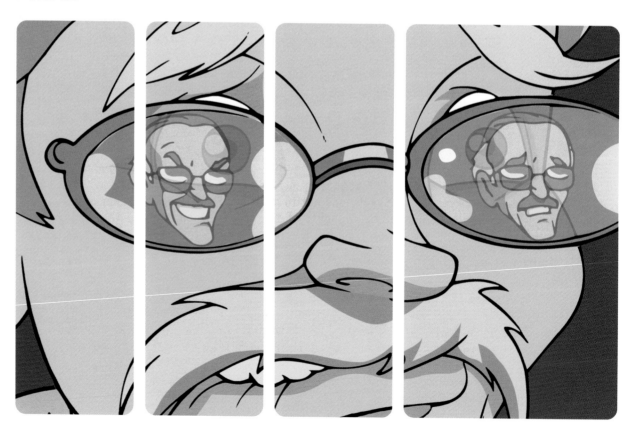

> Born of the married cults of MP3, rock-art, and animation . . . born for the generation of kids addicted to new music and new technology, Flash music videos, and the artistry therein, became a central point for music fans, artists, and technologies.

> Animated, amplified, visual blasts of celebrity and iconography, with hip-hop, metal, pop, and techno narratives, Flash videos took over where MP3s fell short, and excelled where music videos could not go. Flash videos became some sort of in-between solution for visualizing musical experiences on the prebroadband Net. Flash videos can make sitting in front of a computer a pretty cool experience.

> Legendary recording artists Beck, Chuck D, Devo, Dr. Dre, Duran Duran, Kool Keith, Madonna, Phish, The Cure, Todd Rundgren, and even the immortal sounds and images of Pink Floyd and Jimi Hendrix, set Flash and the Internet on fire at the beginning of the millennium. New media never had it so good. We had a blast carving out this niche at Shockwave.com, and an audience quickly started to follow the flow of incredible songs, styles, stories, and vibes. The range of musical and visual styles that appeared in such a short period of time was way over the top.

> These projects were in the expert, experimental hands of visual and interactive masters who were working at creative hothouses such as Bluish and Galle in London; Pixelwurld, Fullerene, and Magritte's Cow in Los Angeles; Alinear, Sudden Industries, and Bullseye Art in Manhattan.

> These new tools also gave newer recording artists a chance to get in front of the same audiences as Madonna and Dr. Dre. The Supreme Beings of Leisure, The Control Group, Jim's Big Ego, The National Joy Band, and Aerial all seized the opportunity to further break themselves to the world, and produced music videos with Flash for their fledgling acts. Of course, none of this would have happened without the insane wizardry of the folks on the Flash team at Macromedia, who built such revolutionary tools.

> During the few short years leading up until the huge "dot-com bubble" burst, tens of millions of dollars were spent commissioning original narratives, games, greeting cards, Web sites, and music videos in order to capture the fancy (and of course the e-mail addresses) of hopefully lucrative audiences. While the dollars have not added up for media companies or venture capitalists behind this explosion, the benefit to fans of pop art is undeniable. Inspired new styles, techniques, and technologies have forever re-rendered and amplified the art of music packaging, promotion, poster art, and music videos in this unique, vector-intensive period.

> The images and words that Stuart and Laurie have collected reflect the efforts of a far-flung group of talent, working toward a collective vision in an insanely turbulent time. This unique book is the result of the passionate work of many producers, designers, illustrators, engineers, new-media gurus, and a few zillion lawyers . . . oh yeah, and not to mention, Flash itself. It keeps on screaming along. The pages that follow capture the thoughts of the artists, their take on the medium, the expression, and the future.

> peter caban, music producer for shockwave.com

> Everything you know about music design is wrong. The paradigm has shifted. Flash has completely eclipsed the traditional method of graphic design. The album cover art of the '20s, '60s, and '80s, although beautiful and inspirational, is nearly the tip of the iceberg when you compare it to the members of this new generation and what they have created. Within the leaves of this book are brilliant examples of edgy, funny, psychedelic, and post–"fuck you" animations. I know that this book will be used as a reference guide of today's designers and animators for years to come.

> three, design director for mtv.com

> By the time we began the project "Yer Fast" the term "Flash video" was already used to refer to a growing body of examples, especially the work exhibited on Shockwave.com. Although I found these pioneering efforts intriguing, most lacked the discipline that I had accumulated while working on music videos intended for broadcast.

> With Flash, as with pre-Flash media, technical and stylistic boundaries must be established before the creative work begins. If this does not happen, some unfortunate things may result. For example, many Flash video producers adopt a bitmap-heavy approach to the video component that ultimately requires them to compress the audio to the point of unintelligibility. This method is not cool with me. Flash videos are musical presentations, after all.

> The other common shortcoming of some Flash artists is a lack of dynamic sensibility. So many Flash videos exhaust their imagery before reaching the halfway point of the song, forcing the viewer to watch the same content multiple times and thus diminishing any desire to watch again.

> For this medium to transcend its novelty, artists need a commitment of a different kind; they need to be willing to subjugate the "fun" aspects of this accessible tool to a more traditional and objective standard based on personal vision, skill, and discipline. Just because using the medium is easy does not mean that producing good work is easy.

> todd rundgren


> Flash is a great tool. It is fairly easy to learn (programming aside); it is ubiquitous on the Internet, which means people do not have to go cruising for plug-ins anymore; and it downloads quickly. It is flexible, versatile, and economical both in bandwidth and affordability. It is a hybrid between cel animation (frame-by-frame drawings) and a motion-graphics tool, which means the work created with Flash will be as varied as its creators' imaginations. Flash lends itself to a spectrum of temperaments, too: from the impatient to the obsessive. It can be used to produce very handmade-drawing-like frame-by-frame animations, and it just as easily can be used to create fluid, mechanical motion-graphics sequences. I like to modulate between both of these realms. And because in Flash a creator controls the components of a scene or frame as a set of objects, refinement is a relatively easy task. In my own work this allows me to do rough sketches and "drill down" into a scene as the art develops.

> I respond to the flat, smooth vector graphics, which are more akin to silk-screen than to digital art (read: airbrush/layers/bitmap/Photoshop). I also respond to being able to use both the handmade, painstaking frame-by-frame techniques and the tweens of fluid computer/motion graphics.

> Flash art is a new medium with strong ties to traditional cartooning. It is a moving, silk-screened, 2-D universe. Years ago Photoshop produced the dominant vernacular that we identify as "digital art," which involves soft edges, transparencies, and layers ("because you can"). Likewise, Flash is starting to have a few "looks" that people identify as the medium. But that is just precedent, not the extent. Flash, like Photoshop, can be likened to a pencil. It is the creator, not the tool, who brings the look.

> I do not put Flash in a corner by itself, just as I do not put oil painting or 16-mm filmmaking into discrete compartments. The uniqueness of Flash as a breakthrough medium lies in its ability to quickly deliver motion graphics and animation over the Internet. This means a much wider audience may see artworks than before, when venues for art—especially experimental film—were limited to a very small number of art houses and museums. In addition, more work is being made and distributed because Flash is cheap to buy and easier to learn than most tools for animation and motion graphics. Flash has begun to influence the look of cutting-edge television graphics—MTV, for instance, uses a lot of vector-looking graphics, and by nature, *South Park* could have been created in Flash.

> marina zurkow

> Today computers are more powerful than ever, and Internet access speeds are accelerating. The broadband of today will become the modem of tomorrow, outmoded by technologies that will see ever-richer media being delivered to a wider variety of devices: TVs, cinemas, wristwatches, perhaps even toasters. Flash is well placed to be at the forefront of this evolution.

> While film and video are still the undisputed rulers of motion, the images they produce are firmly based on what a camera can see in the real world. Flash, on the other hand, was created of the digital universe, allowing a wide range of "never seen before" narrative and stylistic opportunities. We repeatedly find that the most impressive and absorbing digital art we see on the Internet today has been created with the limitations of the computer and the network in mind.

> The artists using Flash to enable their visions today will, in time, be seen as the pioneers of a medium as powerful as graphics, music, and film.

> mark griffiths

> In creating the Vmation for Kittie we really tried to capture the rage and excitement of a live performance. The emphasis was on the backbeat at all times. All the loops and movements were incrementally enhanced to accentuate the beat, resulting in an exaggerated throbbing effect. Also, during the entire production of the Vmation, I wore lipstick and leopard-skin tights to stay in the Kittie "feel."

> david mcmanus

> sudden industries > flash artist: david mcmanus > music artist: kittie > song: brackish

> 11

> In The Getaway People's "Six Pacs" Vmation there is a strong theme based on modes of travel that was inspired by the lyrics of the song. Since performance footage was limited, we used various other visual sources to convey this theme: video and photo stills of buildings, hamburgers, people walking, trucks driving, cars, etc. The flow of the song itself was very important; the tempo of the music dictated the tempo of the imagery and the "style" of motion. Overall, the look and feel of the Vmation was essential as we tried to create a video that reflected the playful nature of the song and the band.

> asif mian

› sudden industries › flash artist: asif mian › music artist: the getaway people › song: six pacs

> It was compelling to work with an archetype artist like Hendrix. His sound is timeless and crosses lines, but is also distinctly molded. This presented some unique circumstances. We wanted to create something indigenous to digital art while laying obvious connection to the style and culture of Hendrix. The piece is an interactive experience that feels like you've stepped into the mind of a computing device that adores Hendrix. I'm left only to hope he is sitting somewhere going "fuck yeah . . ." over at least some aspect of the finished piece.

> neil voss

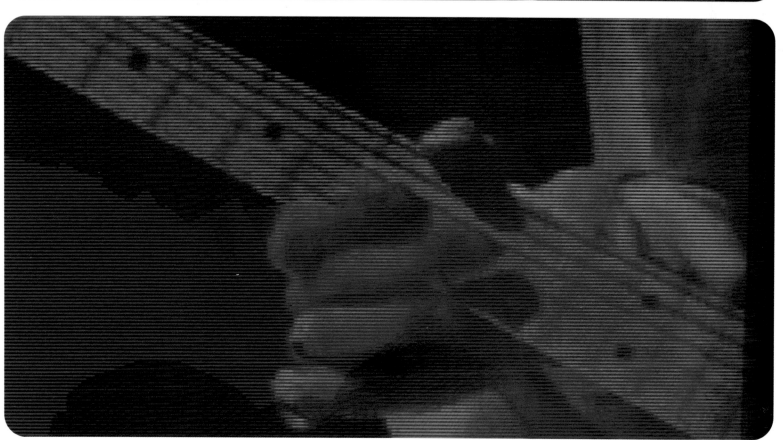

> There is a vibe and an art form to Flash, but ultimately it is limitless. It is an animation tool that just grew from the Web and has this interactive element. Like with other animation programs, you can do anything you want with Flash. Even though it is interactive at its core, you cannot just rely on Flash. You have to be a multidisciplined artist to get good results.

> The Flash look is like a renaissance of older-style graphics from the '60s and '70s. It is up to each artist to grow with the medium and to push him-or herself and to learn. As Flash keeps getting bigger, we will be able to do more with it as artists.

> mike hand

> fullerene productions > flash artist: mike hand > music artist: duran duran > song: someone else not me

DRE

> fullerene productions > flash artist: mike hand > music artist: dr. dre > song: still d.r.e.

> "Braingirl" is an episodic series that chronicles the adventures of a mutant-cute superheroine who wears her insides on the outside. Part cartoon, part experimental film, it utilizes nonconventional elements—such as clip art, rave graphics, and a visually challenging heroine—to comprise its animated nature.

> The story of "Braingirl" accumulates like a snowball—adding detail, circling back, and getting thicker as the viewer sees more. This aggregate narrative is accomplished through formal devices, callbacks, and repetition, as well as traditional linear passages of storytelling.

> marina zurkow

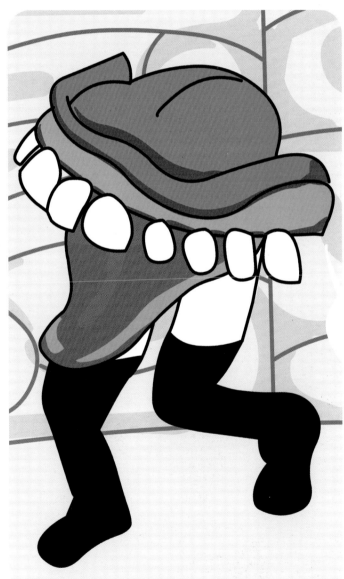

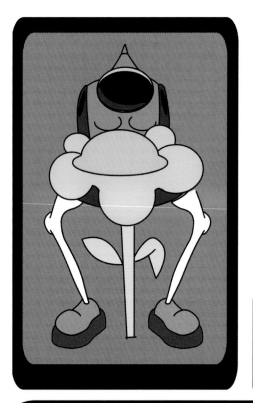

INHALE DEEPLY

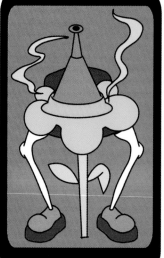

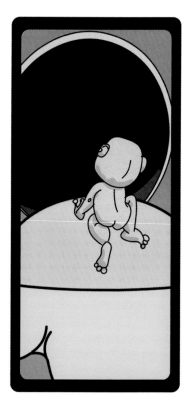

GODDAMN TOURISTS SUCKING UP THE LAST REMAINING SMELL

YOU BIG SMELL SUCKER

> "Funnelhead," which is in development, is the futuristic story of a junk-yard girl mostly made of inorganic parts. The feature-length work tracks her forays in genetics and postconsumer waste. The look and feel of "Funnelhead" is intended to be epic: Flash-meets-Technicolor.

> marina zurkow

> "Little Miss No" is a twelve-minute Flash film about a little girl who learns to say "no." The film is influenced by the graphic sensibility of Paul Rand, and incorporates not only vector graphics, but also collaged, bitmap elements.

> marina zurkow

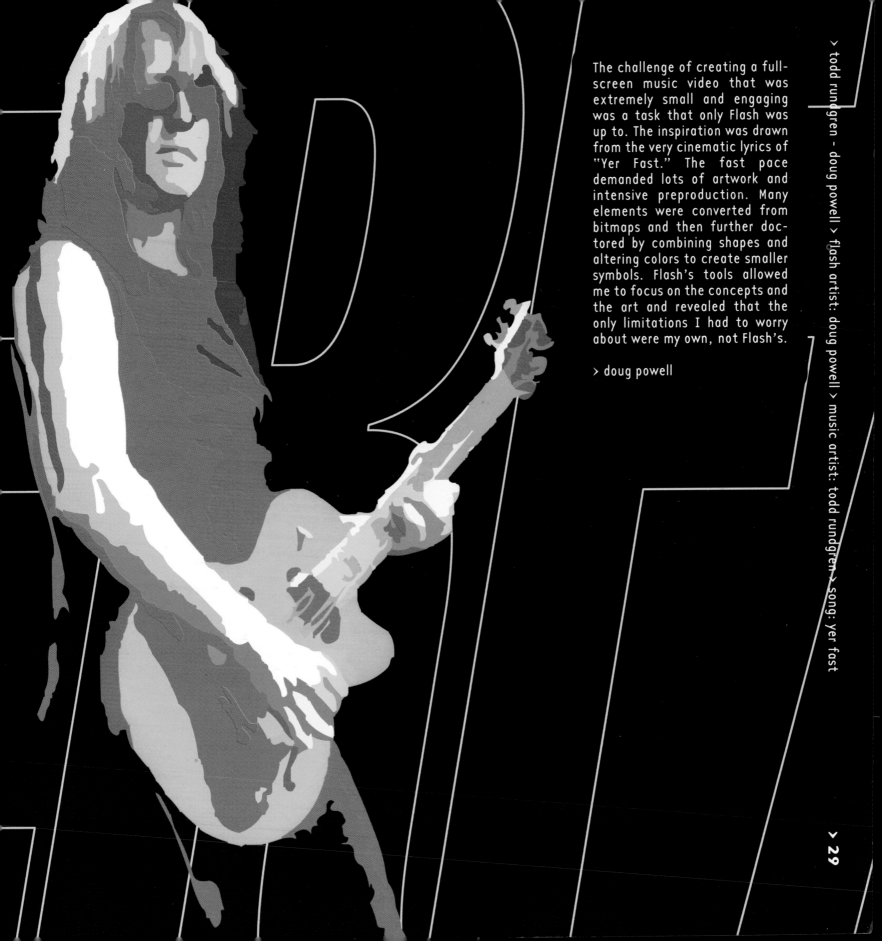

The challenge of creating a full-screen music video that was extremely small and engaging was a task that only Flash was up to. The inspiration was drawn from the very cinematic lyrics of "Yer Fast." The fast pace demanded lots of artwork and intensive preproduction. Many elements were converted from bitmaps and then further doctored by combining shapes and altering colors to create smaller symbols. Flash's tools allowed me to focus on the concepts and the art and revealed that the only limitations I had to worry about were my own, not Flash's.

> doug powell

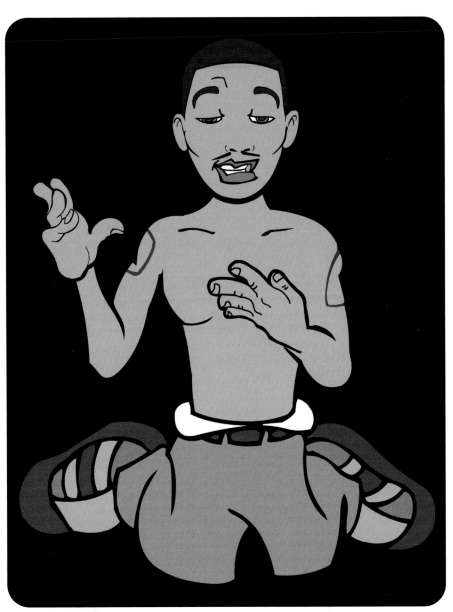

> "Slam Box" was produced in conjunction with Youth Speaks, a nonprofit organization dedicated to young writers based in San Francisco and New York. This unique combination of animation and poetry features some of the nation's most talented spoken-word artists.

> For "Slam Box" the main goal was simply to do justice to these great spoken-word performances, create a visual framework that did not decrease the impact or vitality of the poetry. Since we were building from established pieces of work, our scheme was to create animation using imagery that was visceral and evocative as well as complementary to what was being said. The one element that we did add to the mix was the threads of story that can be detected throughout both pieces, which we thought created a more accessible, conclusive feel to the whole thing.

> adrian baker

> Flash art is a type of hypermedia expression. It allows people to instantly receive a message or conceptual idea through the computer-generated motion graphics and audio, and also allows them to simultaneously respond to this expression. The aesthetic value of Flash is not the application itself. Because it helps the artist to elaborate on good ideas and enhance the quality of his or her work, it is a tool that helps artists execute their visions.

> It is not hard to imagine that Flash will become a popular tool in the future, a mainstream or a distinctively executed style for different channels, such as TV, film, MTV, or hypermedias like the Web. Actually it is already subtly immersed in our daily lives. Madonna's MTV "Music" is a good example that MTV is no longer only available on your "picture box," but is on your personal computer as well. It creates a hyperspace for the audiences that allows them to access their favorite idol more directly. It represents a new form of language and technology, and also brings out a new attitude for the young generation. We can directly gain information globally, timelessly, and interactively.

> ellis lee

> It is amazing how focused your Flash design can get once you decide to use the limitations of the Web as your allies—rather than your enemies—in the work of clear, cogent communication. At least that has been my experience. The spots featured here were all a bit more "wow" in the early stages of their design, but to make them work on narrowband we had to identify elements that did not support the design message and yank them. Sometimes that can be hard because you convince yourself that all of the "wow" has to be in there and the spot will fall apart without it. Worse, you start to believe that your client will not be "blown away" enough. But in the end the "wow" is just wasted space between your message and your audience. As Hemingway once said, "Write the story, take out all of the good lines, and see if it still works." Those are words to live and design by.

> hillman curtis

motion is the message

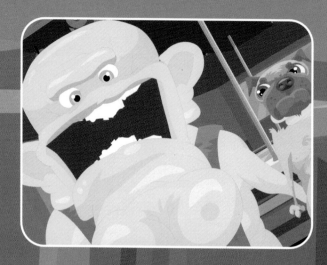

**Today**

> "Nipple Man" is one of our latest attempts to push the limitations of Flash as an animation medium. Our goal has always been to make Flash not look like Flash. We are getting close with "Nipple Man" by animating at close to thirty frames per second, and by getting involved in creating larger-scale productions, both in terms of length and detail. One of the exemplary things about this cartoon is the music by Tim Panella. It not only achieves the silly mood I was looking for, but also gives the piece a cinematic cliff-hanger feel.

> "Napster Bad" was a very simple concept in terms of theme, animation, and length. It was designed purely as a quicky one-off that we could use to encourage viewers to e-mail it around to their friends. Amazingly, this one little toon revolution-ized Camp Chaos in ways I never could have possibly imagined from a visibility and career standpoint. Although I have received thousands of e-mails praising the animation, I feel as if this cartoon is less about animation technique and more about effective uses of Flash as a mass-market tool for making statements about current events.

> bob cesca

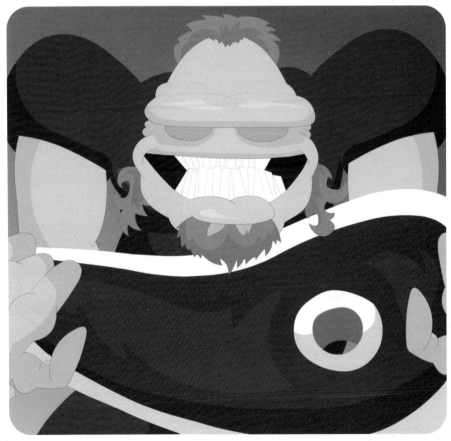

> The "Wish You Were Here" Web film was designed in seven or eight separate parts, which were joined at the end of the project. Despite the fact that such a notion is regarded as a sacrilege in some quarters, the edit consisted of noticeably different sections for the different songs on the original. Floyd asked that the film be referential to the original imagery of the album cover (burning man, diving man, red veil, faceless businessman). The first idea to materialize was the border, which echoed the use of borders on the album cover (where they were white) and made the whole video frame seem bigger on the Web. All borders came from the four elements—earth, air, fire, and water.

> The opening section derived from the sound of wind, from the veil image, from the sand through which the swimmer in the desert was struggling. The next section—the flying hands for "Welcome to the Machine"—was based on black-and-white drawings that described how the shaking hands from the album sticker may have come to meet.

> The next section for "Have a Cigar," a short sequence about masks—particularly the inside-out mask, which seemed to suit the lyrics better—was filmed on DVC, converted to vector graphics, and imported into Flash, where every frame was hand-optimized.

> The actual "Wish You Were Here" part was filmed as a short montage, first to illustrate the song ("two lost souls swimming in a fishbowl"), and second as a mandala to save on digital space as well as appearing attractive. Tilting the camera forty-five degrees was the key. The four-way mandala also reflected the "fourness" of the entire album package—four elements, four sides, four band members, four words to the title and so on.

> The geometric sequence for "The Shine On" verse was executed directly in Flash. The intention was that such a geometric style would be diamondlike, prismlike, and waterlike. The burning picture of the burning man was our little head joke.

> The last part of the Web film was about Syd Barrett. It was meant to be a graphic piece, another kind of visual approach, but mostly it needed to echo the sad, haunting music. I had always agreed that the actual end of the original album would also be the actual end of the Web film. Wish You Were Here, Syd.

> storm thorgerson

> bluish > director: storm thorgerson > flash artist: mark griffiths > music artist: pink floyd > song: wish you were here

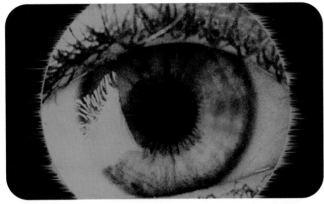

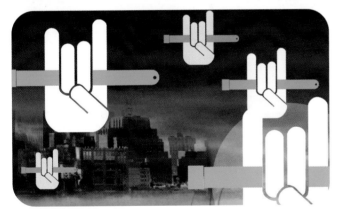

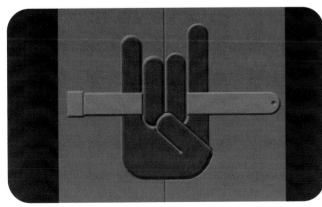

> The Apartment 26 song "Basic Breakdown" is a steady, hard-rock journey into the depths of dementia. From the album entitled *Hallucinating*, the song seemed to be inviting the listener to witness the mental darkness of a nervous breakdown. Hollywood Records agreed with this take on it, and we set out to provide a visual accompaniment to the musical madness. The album cover features a distorted figure standing in the foreground of a red-skied, postnuclear cityscape. Hollywood suggested the idea of moving into the city and beginning the trip with that image. We took it from there, having the official Apartment 26 icon lead us through a dark maze, going deeper and deeper into the subconscious. Among the disturbing imagery and graphics, we used distorted and manipulated live shots of the band aggressively rocking out. It is, after all, about the band. The nightmare vision begins and ends by traveling through the eye of the lead singer, going through a steel door (influenced mostly by the "Get Smart" opening), and flying into the postapocalyptic landscape. This movement provides momentum to get the blood flowing, and adds a sense of closure at the end. Nice bookends.

kirk skodis

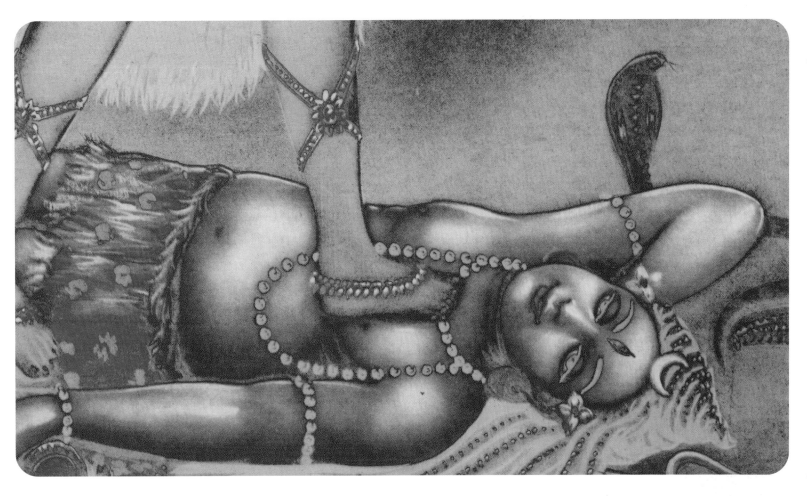

> When Hollywood Records came to us with Diffuser's "Karma," they wanted something different than what they were seeing on Shockwave.com. They wanted to move away from the vector, trace-bitmap look and go for something more grainy, edgy, and bitmappy. I delved into Hindu religious art for obvious reasons. I have always appreciated that art, and really wanted to incorporate it without demeaning it. Of course, the sacred cow is fair game. The song is fun and upbeat, and I didn't get the feeling that the band took it too seriously. Then, armed with band assets (album art, photos, etc.) we roughed in a loose structure (verse, chorus, etc.) and let the song guide us. Often it is this process that leads to something real artistically. Storyboard just what you need, then let yourself "get into it," so to speak. That is when I really enjoy the creation process. That is when four hours pass without you realizing it.

> kirk skodis

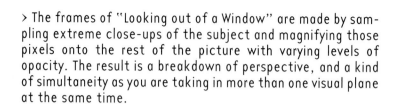

> The frames of "Looking out of a Window" are made by sampling extreme close-ups of the subject and magnifying those pixels onto the rest of the picture with varying levels of opacity. The result is a breakdown of perspective, and a kind of simultaneity as you are taking in more than one visual plane at the same time.

> I do not really see the point in limiting yourself to computer screens. The flash "movement" is surely about more than just a medium that has suddenly become financially accessible. To me it is about liberating creativity.

> I like playing with the fabric, the stuff digital media is made of. You often hear about filmmakers, for example, who try to make the viewers "forget" they are watching a film, because they feel a lack of realism would weaken the experience. I believe the opposite is true: the fabric of the medium does not weaken the experience, it strengthens it. So many accepted idiosyncracies in film, even the simplest cut, surely must remind filmmakers that telling a story is not about creating something realistic, but something mnemonic.

> alexander galle

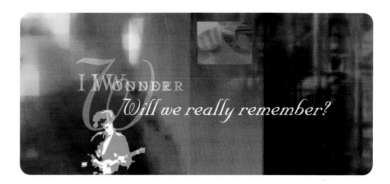

> There's a line in The Cure's song "Out of This World" that totally captures this moment and, I believe, this whole new epoch: "When we look back at it all as I know we will, you and me wide-eyed, I wonder *will we really remember how it feels to be this alive?*"

> alexander galle

> I have been doing the Mr. Man series (which is shown on the following spread) for more than two years now and it is the thing that I am most proud of doing in my long and varied animation career.

> As inspiration, I tend to lean toward the surrealists. The subconscience and dreams are very important to me. While creating Mr. Man I try to tap into these unknown areas, letting the ideas find me.

> It is only after I have finished an animation that I can step back and try to make sense of it all. My thinking is that if I can surprise myself, hopefully I can surprise others.

> "Speedaction" is a collaborative piece between myself and Mars Martin (the composer). Basically, he fed me random ideas and images (bikers, desert, girls from outer space) and I used them as inspiration to create a linear story line.

> Or at least I tried to . . .

> steve whitehouse

"A FEW SHORT WEEKS AND SHE'S A CHAT ROOM SUPERSTAR."

Candy

"EVERYBODY WANTS A PIECE OF CANDY"

"EVERYBODY WANTS A PIECE OF CANDY"

"EVERYBODY WANTS A PIECE OF CANDY NOW."

"MONEY'S TIGHT, YEAH, SHE'S ON AN ALLOWANCE."

> The creative inspiration for this piece came from Nikki Sixx (bass player of 58 and Mötley Crüe), and directly from a song he wrote. I just provided images to follow his lyrics. He had given me and the record company ideas for the look of "Candy," and it took me about five drawings to get her "right." Once I did, then it was off to the races!

> scott pentzer

> While I was doing the "Candy" comic for 58, I kept thinking how cool it would be to do a whole comic on a Web site with some real extensive animation and Flash elements added to the panels. It could be really cool, with sounds and everything, almost like watching a cartoon. I think the more the technology continues, the quicker it will get to a point where it does not take as much memory, and will be much more seamless.

> The 58 "Candy" project was originally envisioned as a four-panel weekly comic strip. However, I knew Nikki Sixx was interested in having as much movement as possible on the Web site. I suggested animating portions of each panel and created animated gifs for the 58 site.

> shaun pollitt

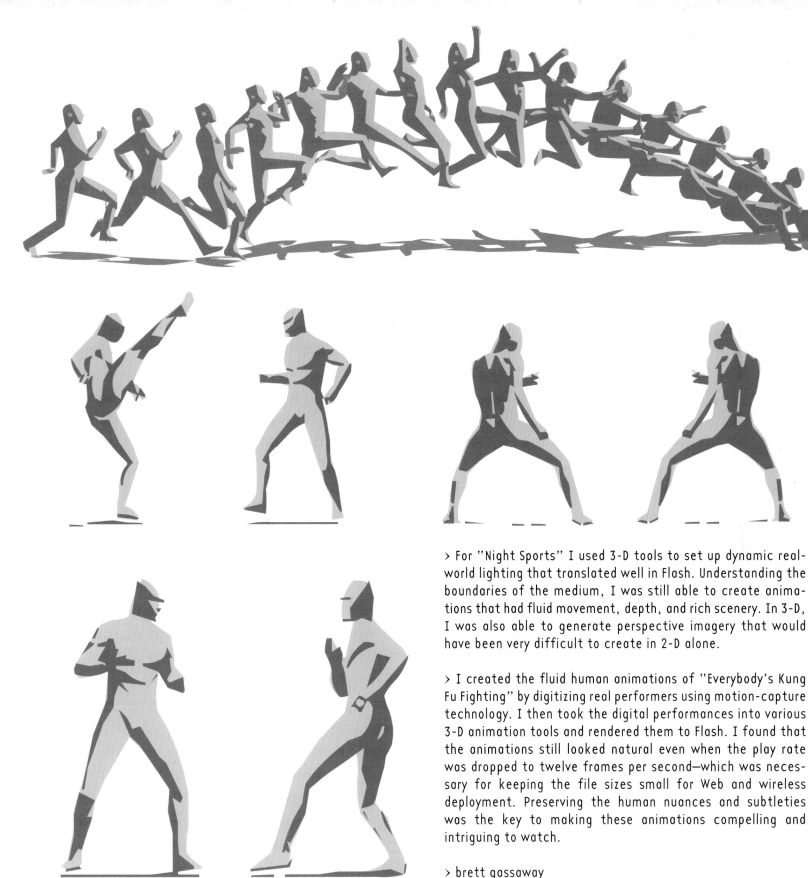

> For "Night Sports" I used 3-D tools to set up dynamic real-world lighting that translated well in Flash. Understanding the boundaries of the medium, I was still able to create animations that had fluid movement, depth, and rich scenery. In 3-D, I was also able to generate perspective imagery that would have been very difficult to create in 2-D alone.

> I created the fluid human animations of "Everybody's Kung Fu Fighting" by digitizing real performers using motion-capture technology. I then took the digital performances into various 3-D animation tools and rendered them to Flash. I found that the animations still looked natural even when the play rate was dropped to twelve frames per second—which was necessary for keeping the file sizes small for Web and wireless deployment. Preserving the human nuances and subtleties was the key to making these animations compelling and intriguing to watch.

> brett gassaway

> This piece is called "Bonzai." It is about an antagonistic little fly who bugs the shit out of this poor guy in a computer cubical. You'll have to watch the piece to see the ending.

> Having spent a great deal of time droning on about naked wild boar hunting and how beneficial a pair of rusty toenail clippers can be in these kinds of dangerous situations, the radish with whom I had been consulting asked me politely to leave. I immediately did (not wanting to lose my composure). Yet as I departed I was accompanied by an intense paranoia that seemed intent on crushing, if not at least bruising, my self-esteem. I fell to the sidewalk and wept for what seemed like an eternity. Asked by the local police to move along, I did.

> joe shields

> This animation is called "Joe Fish." The premise of this piece is that the viewer/participant (i.e., *you*) has a gerbil with a bad attitude that is lowered into a pirana tank to do a little fishing.

> Constantly plauged by my simple-minded compatriots' need to educate me on the ramifications of stapling one's lower lip to one's forehead, I drew the coffee mug close to my chest and sang of days long past with such hearty rebellion that for just one small moment in time all living creatures knew that they had been forgotten once again. The magnitude of a moment like that is not one I care to be responsible for in the future. No sir.

> joe shields

> I have always made strange drawings and comics and had always wanted to produce my own cartoons. It has been an obsession, or maybe even a disease, since childhood. I relentlessly did my own thing and always made my art. I consistently pushed myself further and further and eventually found myself understanding how cartoons were produced and finally realized Bugs Bunny was not a real person. With this realization, the mystery gone, I further studied traditional methods of animation and comics and produced animations for MTV, Nickelodeon, and a bunch of commercials and music videos with the help of expensive equipment supplied by my corporate patrons. This process developed a good portfolio and reel of slickly produced animatics, but was always deducted from a budget that left my landlord penniless. I knew there must be a better way for everybody involved.

> I have spontaneous bursts of work frenzies, but never could actually sit down and do a frame-by-frame, peg-bar type of animation. I was always seeking shortcuts to make what has been living in my mind. The voices in my head were haunting me constantly; I needed my drawings to speak to me. Now, through the miracle of technology, my visions are possible as an independent animator. The way the program and the computers integrate with simple household appliances has enabled this mad-scientist lab to blossom. Although technology has brought such amazing possibilities, I still relate to my computer as though it is a sixty-four box of crayons with a built-in sharpener that is turbo charged. I continue to push myself creatively to fulfill my dreams and am thankful not only to my friends and family but to those faceless software developers. Power to the people.

> steve marcus

› team chman › flash artists: stephan logier - tony derbomez › title: banjo

> Our original experiences come from Web design, but basically we are all hard gamers, and we have learned a lot by spending nights on LAN games, comparing them and determining what mistakes should be avoided. The evolution of Web design technologies led us to focus on the interactive and multimedia potential of the new media and to develop more and more elaborate online entertainment programs. So we fully exploited our techniques and developed several Flash games.

> In creating "Banja," we paid special attention to the graphics and the visual side. This enabled us to make the results as fluid for the player as for the viewer, who can watch the game like an actual cartoon. The game also integrates technologies specific to 3-D—from 3DS Max to Flash—so as to get a perfect render with both 3-D depth and vector smoothness.

> claire giard

> Cleaning up after the rich and famous can give you a unique perspective on things—especially if your name is Clovis and your duties include caring for the blood-stained halls of The Joe Cartoon Company. Sure, a pureed frog or a rectally propelled gerbil is pretty funny stuff, but at the end of the day, someone has to clean that up.

> mike storey

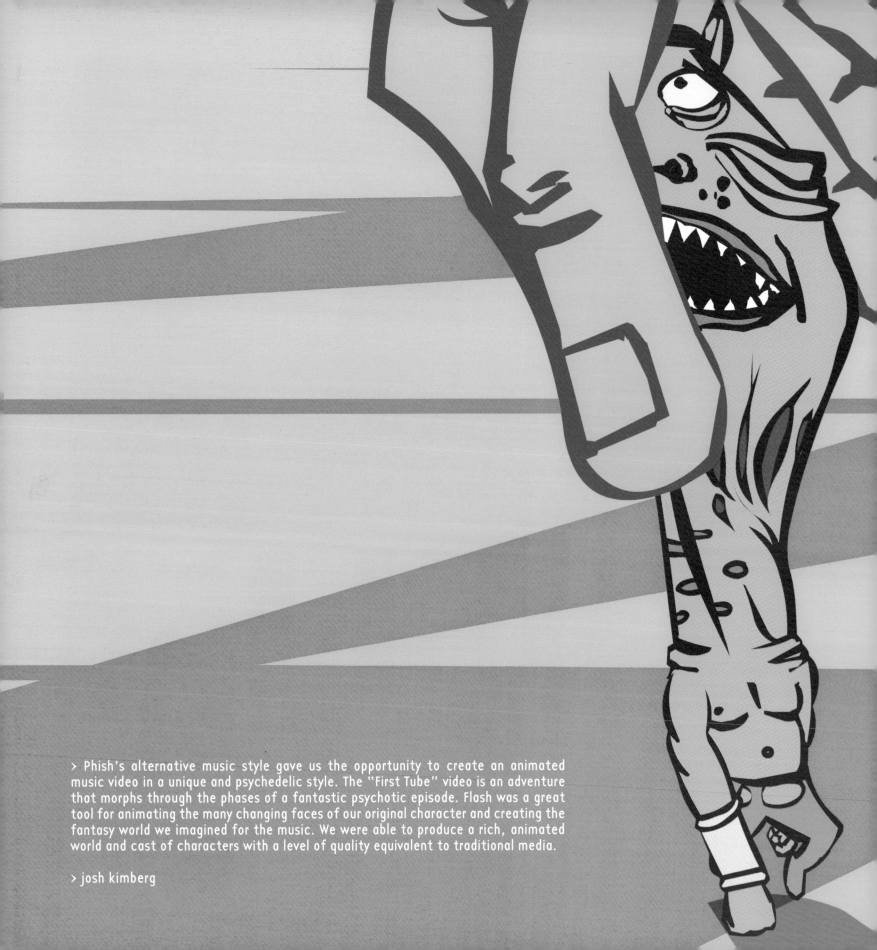

> Phish's alternative music style gave us the opportunity to create an animated music video in a unique and psychedelic style. The "First Tube" video is an adventure that morphs through the phases of a fantastic psychotic episode. Flash was a great tool for animating the many changing faces of our original character and creating the fantasy world we imagined for the music. We were able to produce a rich, animated world and cast of characters with a level of quality equivalent to traditional media.

> josh kimberg

> artmiks [image builders] > flash artist: walter teijgeler > title: underground (part of puree 4)

> Flash created a new take on Web sites and Web experiences. Before Flash we were able to show people images and sounds, sometimes even a combination of both, but we were never able to really combine and synchronize the two. Now we face the challenge of taking sound, image, and movement toward a full experience of the (sur)real Web world. The ability to add user interaction takes it even further. We are always trying to find ways of drawing visitors into our world and surprising them. The two sites shown—www.puree.nl and www.solarvibes.nl—are both designed using an experience rather than retrieving flat information. We feel that if a user experiences the message, it will have a longer duration and have a larger impact.

> marco de boer

> "Kozik's Inferno" was one of those rare opportunities to use cartoon animation in the service of a truly sophisticated conceit, where arcane literary references (chief among them, of course, being the fourteenth-century epic poem, Dante's *Inferno*) were freely mixed with pop art, cartoon slapstick, and a kind of nonparody dark graphic novel worldview. "Inferno" was rock poster artist Frank Kozik's vision of life, death, and everything in between. It became one of those unusual properties that could only have originated in the highly experimental Internet content boom of the last years of the twentieth century. Flash particularly suited Mr. Kozik's art direction, which evolved during years of working with the silk-screen printing process.

> george evelyn

> "The God and Devil Show" is basically a Web-based celebrity roast disguised as a talk show. I focus on creating good likenesses of the guests. That's really my number one artistic concern. Because if the drawings don't look like the celebrities we are parodying, then who are we parodying?

> I think it was Woody Allen who said, "It's pretty or funny, you can't have both." Which is kind of true. Since the main job of "The God and Devil Show" is to be funny, I often sacrifice beauty for a fart joke. Some artist, huh?

> aubrey ankrum

HOLLYWOOD

Julia Roberts is Erin Brockovich

mondo

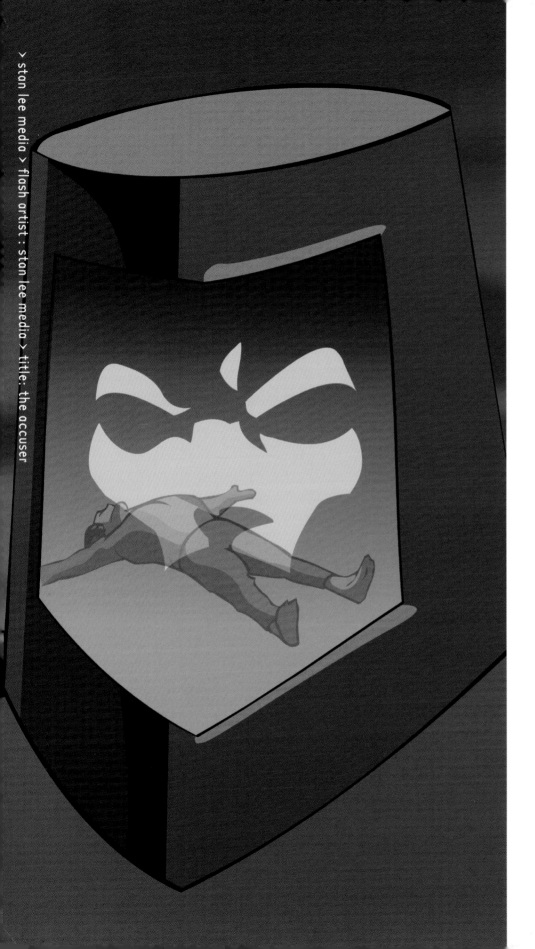

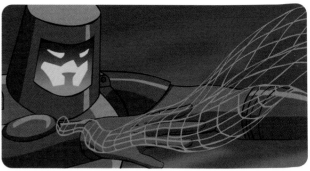

> I have always found that the more I cover a job on all angles and the more control I have of it, the better it is. A lot of people don't want that because they worry that if they make a wrong move, the failure will fall on their shoulders. But you have to have faith in yourself and in what you are doing, know that you are right. The more I can control the project, the less likely someone else is to screw it up.

> With "The Accuser" (which is shown on the left and above), the producers wanted a dark look, but comic book artists handle lighting completely differently now than the way I was taught. The way they color today, every bulge and every muscle has a highlight on it. Where's the light source? There is no light source and that bothers me. You cannot take liberties with lighting. My forte is realism and the lighting and research are very important to my style of art. So I collaborated with the Flash artist to make sure that "The Accuser" had my style of highlights.

> My advice to the young Internet artists today who want to get into it is to hone your technical skills—because the better the artist you are, the better it's going to work for you in every aspect. Norman Rockwell studied for nine years, but then when he started his career he did covers right away. He was a studied, trained technician.

> The attitude of today is that more is better. But with Web animation it can become hard to look at the picture if it is too full. Simple is better.

> I strive for simplicity and realism. As a result people tell me my work is very clear and easy to look at.

> russ heath

> "Thugs on Film" is hosted by Cecil and Stubby, two English working-class "lads" with a healthy appreciation for the movies. Stubby likes them violent with loads of "shagging," whereas Cecil has a more refined understanding of the art of film. Catch the thugs as they review the latest blockbuster release and stay tuned for the movie trivia quiz after each episode.

> Follow Piki and Poko, two anime-inspired teen heroines, as they set out to save StarLand from total chaos. The cosmic StarSisters battle a cast of fantastic characters and mix it up with zodiac DJs along the way. With adventurous story lines and horoscopes that are fun to share, "Piki & Poko" is sure to please any animation fan.

> lourdes alba

› stan lee media › flash artist: stan lee media › title: backstreet project

> With the "I Hear Voices" video, we wanted to capture the gritty, off-kilter style of Doom's lyrics and delivery. Having experience converting imagery into vector artwork, we knew immediately the conversion's rough output would mirror Doom's style. So we translated actual video footage into a series of flat, graphic illustrations, creating a music video that matched the artist's sensibilities, fit well within the vector world of Shockwave.com, and raised the standard for what could be delivered in a small file size online. Doom's video speaks volumes in terms of successfully matching an artist's style to a medium.

> debra mccain

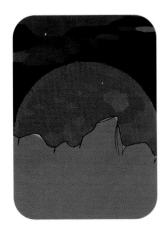

> When working on the "Thin Line Between Raw and Jiggy" video, we drew a lot of inspiration from the world of graffiti art, particularly from the streets of San Francisco, New York City, Los Angeles, and, by way of our Canadian artist, Toronto. We embrace hip-hop culture and the idea of sampling and remixing proven techniques and inventing new ones in an evolving synthesis of artistic form and motion.

> Technology and ideas are merging together at the conceptual stage of development—Flash representing one tool/medium/art form where this new thought process comes to the fore. Flash is a child of the Internet paradigm, a networked understanding of media creation and flow. As the rest of the entertainment world comes to understand the inherent strengths of idea creation within the Internet paradigm, Flash will play a part in both making and wrapping next-level content for network delivery.

> seth fershko

> Creating our video for The Control Group's song "Chemicals" with Flash was exciting but challenging, due to the constraints that were placed upon the file size. Two megs of space for three minutes of animation? No problem. Add three minutes of streaming MP3 audio to that? BIG problem.

> We were forced to impose a serious limit on the number of graphics in the movie, so we spent the bulk of our image budget on four detailed views of our main character and a collection of background scenery. The character's body was assembled in pieces, layered one atop another, with the centers of each limb positioned so that the entire structure functioned like a primitive 2-D IK skeleton. The initial overhead for each piece was great, but we were constantly reusing them in different animated clips throughout the video, at a minimal cost. The layering gave our character an eerie, paper doll-like texture, and we wanted to keep the scenery design consistent with that style. Thus, we imported photographs into Flash, traced them with a very high tolerance level, and optimized them at the maximum setting. The end result was a set of surreal, impressionistic landscapes, which created continuity between the main character and his environment.

> Technical details aside, our goal was to create a plot-driven video that echoed the haunting tone of the song. We wanted to give the viewer a reason to stay with us through the end. By creating an empathetic character, we were hoping to generate some emotional interest in the piece, and leave the audience feeling fulfilled with the outcome of the story.

> andrew king

> The idea behind "Preschool Proto-Cops" was to create a TV-quality Flash cartoon with original characters. It had to have a solid story line, be funny, and feature great artwork and animation. I wanted it to be very smooth and clean with a polished look to everything—something that vector graphics can deliver very well, but suprisingly, you don't see very often.

> Creatively, it was very hard to introduce ten brand-new characters and the premise of the show in only four minutes, but I think it comes across successfully. It really feels like a fully fledged universe that the characters inhabit.

> james hutchinson

> The aesthetic features of the Flash medium that I respond to the most are the cleanliness of the lines and the boldness of the images. That is reflected in the cartoons I draw, which are simple, strong, and clean. I am not sure whether I was drawn to Flash because it would do my illustrations justice, or if I have purposefully simplified my drawing style so the art will look great in Flash.

> "Solar Wind" was created as an online greeting card, so it had to have a message, or sentiment, as well as be entertaining to watch. The idea for it came from an old cartoon I drew, where the Spork character was floating though space. It was in the form of a poem. The ending was: "As I pass Uranus, things get quite dangerous. As buttocks get warmer and warmer . . . watch out! A supernova. I think it is all over. Thus ends my flatulent trauma."

> james hutchinson

> Flash motion media forces the artist to completely optimize his or her creative process and utilize only what is absolutely necessary to convey the thoughts and emotions that the piece dictates. In the creation of "Inertia" I sought to create a seamless experience that did not give the appearance of repetitive loops, but immersed the viewer with organic shapes and textures that flowed in harmony with the track. The piece does, in fact, use many of the same design elements and animations in order to respect file-size limitations, but the elements are used in varying manners each time they are introduced to the stage.

> A major part of the art direction of "Inertia," which sets it apart from most other longer-format Flash pieces, is its use of video. Prior to the production of the piece, we coordinated a very specific video shoot to capture images of the band members. The images were painstakingly filtered down until only the smallest number of frames necessary to convey the vibe of each of the band members was used.

> adam boozer

# NEVER THE SAME

> We wanted the video for "Never the Same" to have a narrative—a plot within the context of the movie trailer. We basically created the entire movie on paper then edited it like a trailer. Movie posters of the '30s, '40s, and '50s inspired the look of the video; in particular we paid homage to the film-graphics king Saul Bass.

> We created a storyboard, then had a day-long shoot in a green-screen studio. After that we began automating the process of importing the files into Flash, coloring them, etc. We wanted the design to be inspired by, but not be a direct rip-off, of that particular genre, so we combined looks and added a different take on it.

> andres moreta

> Todd Rundgren liked Supreme Being of Leisure's "Strangelove Addiction" Flash video and approached us to try an experiment he was working on. He wanted to have real video motion, i.e., thirty frames per second in a Flash video. He had worked on a couple of experiments of rotating objects running at 30fps that streamed on a 56K modem and he wanted us to expand upon them for his song "I Hate My Frickin' ISP." Using his experiments as a starting point, we added our design aesthetic and programming to enhance this promising new Flash technique.

> andres moreta

> The world was becoming boring! Suddenly, Piratenet called the hotline: "Produce three twenty-two-minute Flash animation pieces. We have no scripts and no animators, just inspirational art!" Their secret weapon: a true willingness to experiment. Finally, I could utilize my mystery training from the temple of animation to form three different teams to run three different ways. From "Dream Detective" through "Bludd" and finally "Rolling Redknuckles," we conquered all demons from "traditional" to "Flash" animation. (Insert ad for snack cake of your choice here.) And so, proudly we stand looking over the sunset on the horizon toward our next challenge.

> andrew brandou

> piratenet > artist: robert williams > flash artist: sam egan > title: dream detective

> piratenet > director: danielle marleau > flash artist: andrew brandou > title: bludd

> Heavy.com is an entertainment destination that attempts to give the user a glimpse of what television will eventually become. We have used the latest in Web technology and production software to create an easy-to-use site that takes full advantage of broadband. On the whole the experience has been very positive. Weathering the dot-com storm, we have risen above the rest of online destinations as a viable alternative in entertainment. Not only has this been creatively fulfilling, but it has given us a chance to forge new ground.

> "American Suck Countdown" comments on who is currently sucking the most in the music world. Who is so bad that they're not good, but still just bad? What number comes after 6? These questions are answered in every countdown.

> Heavy is known by the logo of the squatting sumo wrestler. He is featured in several sumo animations, including "Die Sushi Die," "Sumos Kill," and "Sumozilla." In the animations that precede our site we elaborate on the Sumo's character by putting him in familiar and not-so-familiar roles.

> About "Munchy Man & Fatty" . . . just chill, baby. Munchy Man, Fatty, and assorted cohorts are men with a mission, superheroes intent on cleaning up a one-horse town. Resin-scrapers should look elsewhere.

> ryan honey

AMERICAN
**SUCK**
COUNTDOWN

LAUNCH CU

> calliope studios > flash artists: peer bazarini - jean-david boujnah > title: people spaces and things

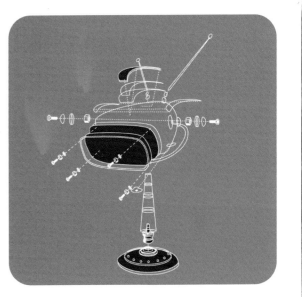

ENT EPISODE

> heavy > flash artist: ryan honey > title: american suck countdown

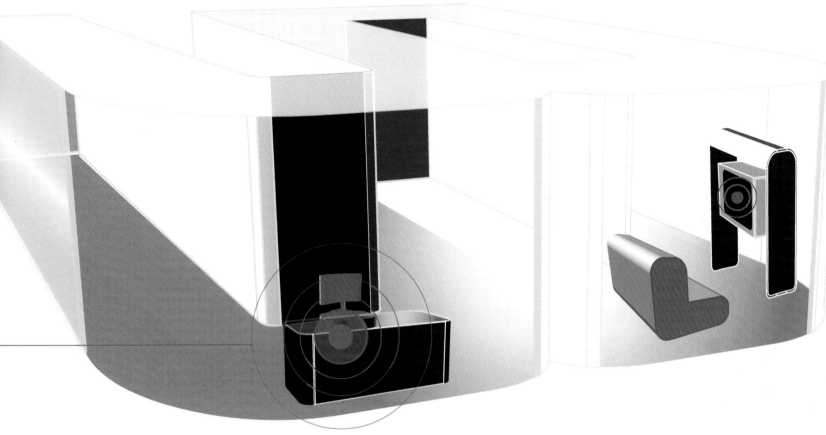

> Making its appearance in the mid-1990s, amidst the surge of our (digitally enhanced) consumer culture, Flash became a means by which artistry could flourish efficiently and effectively on the Web. Though its early interfaces were a bit "unconventional," Flash nonetheless promoted a welcome alternative to the "disposable" corporate dissimilarity to which most Web design was falling victim. Early in its introduction Flash facilitated a revolution of Barlowian stature.

> As digital artists, we combine technology with ingenuity and emotional appeal to elicit response. Today, Flash is the perfect tool. An intuitively organic interface, Flash allows the designer to design from the heart. In turn, Flash sites embody the Internet's natural tendency towards change, transgression, and pragmatic minimalism. The result is aesthetic authenticity—replacing the materialism of the moment with something of lasting substance.

> peer bazarini and jean-david boujnah

> The concept behind Icebox was devised by three of its original founders, John Collier, Howard Gordon, and Rob Lazebnik, who were very successful television writers at the time (the fall of 1999). Icebox was born out of their frustration in not being able to control the creative process. They saw the Internet, and Flash animation, as a tool that would allow them the chance to create content without the usual barriers to entry, such as the cumbersome studio and network development process.

> Flash was this great new—and more importantly, inexpensive—method of animation that allowed a skilled artist to create original cartoons on his or her desktop. The goal of Icebox was to write (with the writer having complete creative control), design, voice, score, and animate a high-quality show that could be marketed directly to the audience via the Internet, all under one roof. In order to realize this vision, a team of writers, producers, designers, and animators was assembled at Icebox. Jerry Richardson headed the design team and Joel Kuwahara headed the production team. Both came from the traditional animation world (*The Simpsons*). They were able to adapt their knowledge to the Flash and Internet worlds in order to assist in the production of twenty-two animated series— including "Hard Drinkin' Lincoln," "Meet the Millers," and "Mr. Wrong"—during their tenure at the original Icebox.

> One of the biggest challenges at the time was bandwidth and file size. Most users were working with 56K modems. If download times were too long, we knew we would lose our audience. Joel and Jerry, along with many of the other artists, developed new techniques in Flash that enabled them to deliver a fully functional Webisode in a one-megabyte file size. This takes less than three minutes to download on a slow modem and provides a satisfying user experience.

> The results speak for themselves. Many of our Webisodes received in excess of a million viewers, with minimal promotion. And more importantly creative boundaries were pushed in all aspects of these shows, from the writing to the artwork to the music. Just as graphic novels advanced comic books as an art form, Flash seems to be advancing animation.

> tal vigderson

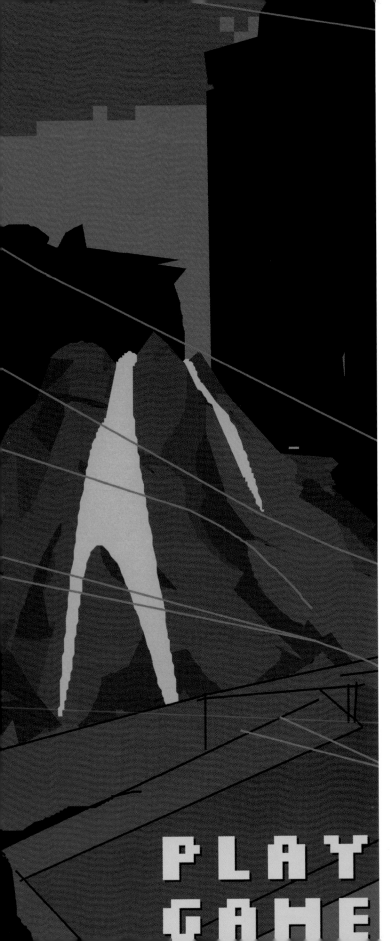

> "Against the Elements" is a song by Confrontation Camp that was written by Chuck D for the X-Games. We wanted to create a video that incorporated a game that was fun to play and that fit into the story line of the video. The video tells the story of the chaos that ensues when the X-Games are invaded by killer storms. In the video a surfer gets picked up out of the water and surfs around in a tornado, a street luger over lava, and a skater in the sky. (Street luge is an off-shoot of skating, skateboarding, and cart racing where the rider lies on a brakeless board and plummets down paved hills at 40 mph.)

> Somewhere in the middle of all this we incorporated a video game in which the user has to dodge objects caught in the tornado. The video was completed in less than three weeks from start to finish. This would not have been possible without Flash.

> ronen lasry and daniel szecket

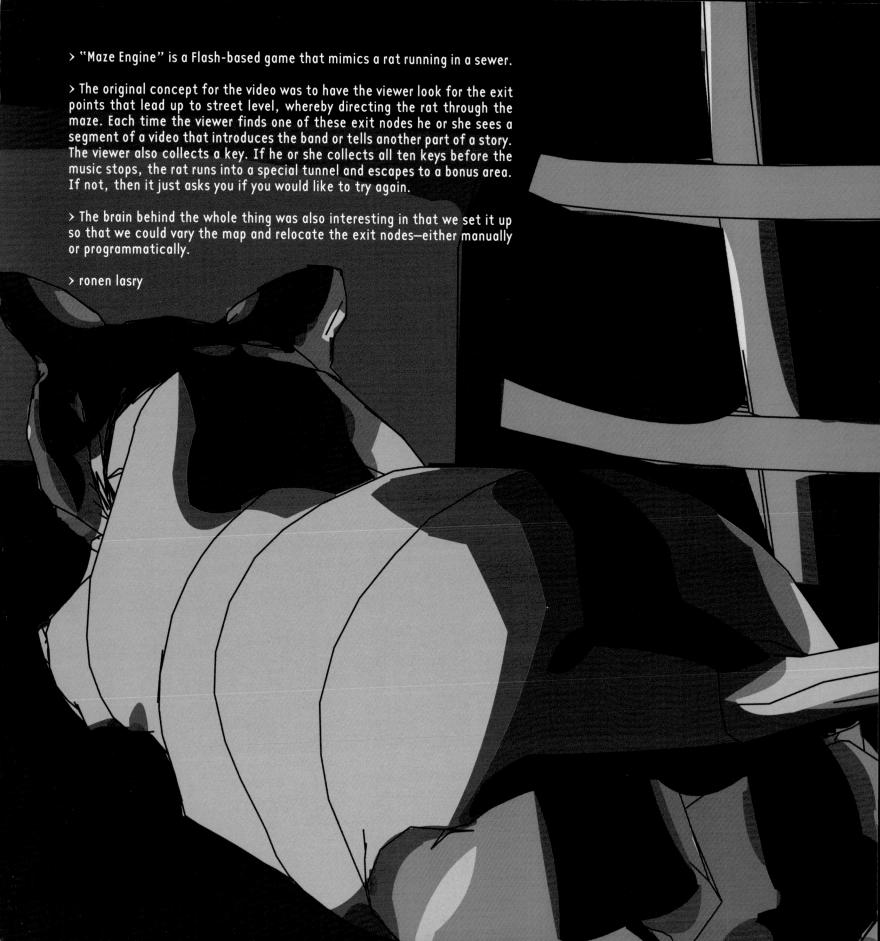

> "Maze Engine" is a Flash-based game that mimics a rat running in a sewer.

> The original concept for the video was to have the viewer look for the exit points that lead up to street level, whereby directing the rat through the maze. Each time the viewer finds one of these exit nodes he or she sees a segment of a video that introduces the band or tells another part of a story. The viewer also collects a key. If he or she collects all ten keys before the music stops, the rat runs into a special tunnel and escapes to a bonus area. If not, then it just asks you if you would like to try again.

> The brain behind the whole thing was also interesting in that we set it up so that we could vary the map and relocate the exit nodes—either manually or programmatically.

> ronen lasry

&gt; magritte's cow &gt; flash artists: daniel szecket - ronen lasry &gt; music artist: alyy &gt; song: maze engine

**3 > JOE CARTOON**
www.joecartoon.com

*Title*
Loading Page of Gerbil Bar 2
*Flash Lead Programmer*
Joe Shields
*Creative Director*
Joe Shields
*Music Artist*
Joe Shields
*Writer*
Joe Shields

**6 > STAN LEE MEDIA**

*Title*
Evil Clone
*Flash Artists*
Stan Lee Media

**9 > JOE CARTOON**
www.joecartoon.com

*Title*
Loading Page of Web Site
*Flash Lead Programmer*
Joe Shields
*Creative Director*
Joe Shields
*Music Artist*
Joe Shields
*Writer*
Joe Shields

**10–13 > SUDDEN INDUSTRIES**
www.suddenindustries.com

*Title*
Brackish
*Flash Artist*
David McManus
*Executive Producers*
Stuart S. Shapiro
Adam Spielberger
*Music Artist*
Kittie
www.kittie.net
*Song*
Brackish
*Record Company*
Artemis Records
www.artemisrecords.com

*Title*
Six Pacs
*Flash Artist*
Asif Mian
www.evaq.net
*Music Artist*
The Getaway People
www.getawaypeople.com
*Song*
Six Pacs

*Record Company*
Columbia Records
www.columbiarecords.com

**14–17 > ALINEAR**
www.alinear.net

*Title*
Purple Haze
*Creative Director*
Neil Voss
*Lead Designer*
Neil Voss
*Lead Programmer*
Neil Voss
*Programming and Design*
Rumi Humprey
Scot Williamson
*Additional Contributors*
Aaron Anderson
Scott Pittinsky
*Producer for Shockwave.com*
Peter Caban
*Producer for MCA Records*
Aaron Foreman
*Music Artist*
Jimi Hendrix
www.jimihendrix.com
*Song*
Purple Haze
*Record Company*
MCA Records/Experience Hendrix
www.mca.com
Jimi Hendrix images © Experience Hendrix L.L.C.

**18–23 > FULLERENE PRODUCTIONS**
www.fullerene.com

*Title*
Still D.R.E.
*Flash Artist*
Mike Hand
*Music Artist*
Dr. Dre
www.drdre.com
*Song*
Still D.R.E.
*Record Company*
Interscope
www.interscope.com

*Title*
Someone Else Not Me
*Flash Artist*
Mike Hand
*Music Artist*
Duran Duran
www.duranduran.com
*Song*
Someone Else Not Me
*Record Company*
Hollywood Records
www.hollywoodrecords.com

*Title*
Earthlink: Magellan

*Flash Artists*
Mike Hand
Mary Evelyn McGough
*Agency*
TBWA/Chiat/Day

*Title*
Nicotine and Gravy
*Flash Artist*
Mike Hand
*Music Artist*
Beck
www.beck.com
*Song*
Nicotine and Gravy
*Record Company*
Interscope
www.interscope.com

**24–27 > O-MATIC CORP/MARINA ZURKOW**
www.o-matic.com
www.thebraingirl.com

*Title*
Braingirl
*Director/Writer*
Marina Zurkow
*Flash Artist*
Marina Zurkow

*Titles*
Funnelhead
Little Miss No
*Flash Artist*
Marina Zurkow
*Writers*
Marina Zurkow
Ceridwen Morris
*Director*
Marina Zurkow

**28–29 > TODD RUNDGREN
DOUG POWELL**
www.patronet.com

*Title*
Yer Fast
*Flash Artist*
Doug Powell
www.dougpowell.com
*Music Artist*
Todd Rundgren
*Song*
Yer Fast
*Record Company*
Artemis Records
www.artemisrecords.com

**30–33> MADLAB CREATIVE**
www.madlabcreative.com

*Title*
Slam Box Episode One, The Ghost
*Creative Director*
Adrian Baker

Director of Animation
Tane Ross
Writer
Antonio Elmo Mims (aka Aman)

Title
Slam Box Episode Two, Unlocked 2000
+ A Cultural Revolution
Creative Director
Adrian Baker
Director of Animation
Tane Ross
Writer
Jason Mateo (aka the Kreative Dweller)

## 34–37 > SCREAM THERAPY
www.screamtherapy.com

Title
Black Transmission
www.screamtherapy.com/
BlackTransmission-Shockwave.html
Flash Artist
Ellis Lee
www.geocities.com/leeelly/opening.html
Music Artist
The Januaries
Producer
Scream Therapy
Song
Black Transmission
Record Company
Foodchain Records
www.foodchainrecords.com

Title
Zip Code
Animator
John Bloom
Writer
Jim Adler
Producer
Scream Therapy

## 38–39 > HILLMAN CURTIS
www.hillmancurtis.com

Title
Hillman Curtis Home Page Animation
Flash Artists
Hillman Curtis
Ian Kovalik
Homera Chaudhry
Matt Horn

## 40–41 > CAMP CHAOS ENTERTAINMENT
www.campchaos.com

Titles
Nipple Man
Napster Bad
Writer/Director/Animator
Bob Cesca

Music
Tim Panella
Backgrounds
Marc Manalli
Voices
Bob Cesca
Producer
Tara Donnon

## 42–47 > BLUISH
www.bluish.com

Title
Wish You Were Here
http://pinkfloyd.shockwave.com
Producer/Director
Storm Thorgerson
www.stormthorgerson.co.uk
Flash Animation and Authoring
Mark Griffiths
Toby Glover
Dulcie Fulton (at Bluish)
Audio Mix
James Guthrie
Camera
Rupert Truman
Video Editor
Richard Shaw (at Swordfish)
Drawings
Finlay Cowan
Assistant
Catherine Campbell
Music Artist
Pink Floyd
www.pinkfloyd.com
Song
Wish You Were Here
Record Company
Capitol Records
www.hollywoodandvine.com/pinkfloyd

## 48–51 > REAL PIE MEDIA
www.realpie.com

Title
Basic Breakdown
Flash Artist
Kirk Skodis
Music Artist
Apartment 26
www.hollywoodrecords.com/apartment26
Song
Basic Breakdown
Record Company
Hollywood Records
www.hollywoodrecords.com

Title
Karma
Flash Artist
Kirk Skodis
Music Artist
Diffuser
www.hollywoodrecords.go.com/diffuser

Song
Karma
Record Company
Hollywood Records
www.hollywoodrecords.com

## 52–53 > GALLE
www.galle.com

Title
Girl Looking Out of a Window
Artist
Alexander Galle
Model
Monica Masias

Title
Out of This World
Flash Artist
Alexander Galle
Music Artist
The Cure
www.thecure.com
Song
Out of This World
Record Company
Elektra
http://elektra.com

## 54–57 > WHITEHOUSE ANIMATION INC.
www.whitehouseanimationinc.com

Title
Speedaction
Flash Artist
Steve Whitehouse
Music Artist
3 Peace
www.whirldrecords.com/rock
Song
Speedaction
Record Company
Whirld Records
www.whirldrecords.com

Title
Mr. Man
Flash Artist
Steve Whitehouse

## 58–59 > AMERICOMA RECORDS/BEYOND MUSIC
www.beyondmusic.com
www.americoma.com

Title
Piece of Candy
Illustrator/Artist
Scott Pentzer
Production/Flash Artist
Shaun Pollitt
Art Director
Susan McEowen
Music Artist
58

www.58music.com
*Song*
Piece of Candy
*Record Company*
Americoma Records/Beyond Music

**60–61 > HOUSE OF MOVES**
www.moves.com

*Titles*
Night Sports
Everybody's Kung Fu Fighting
*Flash Artist*
Brett Gassaway
www.characterspot.com

**62–63 > JOE CARTOON**
www.joecartoon.com

*Title*
Bonzai
*Flash Lead Programmer*
Joe Shields
*Creative Director*
Joe Shields
*Music Artist*
Joe Shields
*Writer*
Joe Shields

*Title*
Joe Fish
*Flash Lead Programmer*
Joe Shields
*Creative Director*
Joe Shields
*Music Artist*
Joe Shields
*Writer*
Joe Shields

**64–67 > DESTOON – STEVE MARCUS**
www.smarcus.com

*Title*
Jails, Hospitals & Hip-Hop
*Flash Artist*
Steve Marcus
*Co-Animator*
Corey Shaw
*Music Artist*
Danny Hoch

**68–69 > TEAM CHMAN**
www.teamchman.com

*Title*
Banja
www.banja.com
*Flash Artist*
Tony Derbomez
*Flash Lead Programmer*
Stephan Logier
*Music Artist/Sound Designer*
Gauthier Malou

*Title*
Mutafukaz
*Flash Artist*
Guillaume "Run" Renard

*Title*
My Dear Billy
*Flash Artist*
Sebastien "Rolito" Giuli

**70–71 > GOONLAND**
www.goonland.com

*Title*
Sweepin' Joe's
*Flash Artist/Programmer*
Mike Storey

**72–73 > BULLSEYE ART**
www.bullseyeart.com

*Title*
First Tube
*Executive Producer*
Josh Kimberg
*Creative Director/Flash Artist*
Nick Cogan
*Senior Content Developer*
Ryan Edwards
*Interactive Design*
Dan Kellner
*Animation*
Ryan Edwards
Efrain Cintron
Peter Rida Michail
Dan Kellner
Bob Strang
*Music Artist*
Phish
www.phish.com.
*Song*
First Tube
*Record Company*
Elektra
www.elektra.com

**74–75 > ARTMIKS [IMAGE BUILDERS]**
www.artmiks.nl

*Title*
Underground (Part of Puree 4)
www.puree.nl
*Flash Artist*
Walter Teijgeler
*Senior Creative Director*
Marco de Boer
*Title*
solarvibes
www.solarvibes.nl
*Flash Artist*
Marco de Boer
*Flash Programers*
Vincent Poeze
Michael Nieuwenhuizen

*Senior Creative Director*
Marco de Boer

**76–77 > WILDBRAIN**
www.wildbrain.com

*Title*
Kozik's Inferno
www.mansruin.com
*Art Director*
Frank Kozik
*Creative Director*
George Eveyln
*Flash Lead Programmer*
Ty Bardi
*Executive Producer*
Amy Capen

*Title*
Joe Paradise
*Flash Artist/Graphic Creative Director*
Roque Ballesteros
*Flash Lead Programmer*
Bill Hunt
*Producer*
Amy Capen
www.wildbrain.com

**78–81 > MONDO MEDIA**
www.mondomedia.com

*Title*
The God and Devil Show
*Flash Artist*
Aubrey Ankrum

*Title*
Thugs on Film
*Flash Artist*
Aubrey Ankrum
*Writer/Director*
Kamau Bell

*Title*
Piki & Poko
*Flash Artist*
Aubrey Ankrum
*Creators*
Mark Ewert
David Cutler
*Art/Animation Director*
Kelley Lamsens

**82–87 > STAN LEE MEDIA**

*Title*
Evil Clone
*Flash Artists*
Stan Lee Media
*Title*
The Accuser
*Creative Producer/Director*
Larry Houston

Artists
Armando Gil
Paula LaFond
Jo Luna
Lou Scarborough
Scott Koblish
Oscar Lopez
Majella Milne
John Statema
*Digital Artist Supervisor*
Zachary Foley
*Lead Digital Artists*
Damon O'Keefe
Sibyl Wickersheimer
*Digital Artists*
Michael Hood
Justin Murphy
Linda Tomarchio
Spencer Laudiero
Damon O'Keefe
Monika Zech

*Title*
7th Portal
*Art Director*
Arron Sowd
*Lead Artist*
Scott Koblish
*Artists*
Claude Denis
Armando Gil
Oscar Lopez
Allan Fernando
Paula La Fond
Don Manuel
*Digital Artist Supervisor*
Zachary Foley
*Lead Digital Artist*
Peter Choe
*Digital Artists*
Brian Burks
Tim Burlingame

*Title*
Backstreet Project
*Art Director*
Arron Sowd
*Lead Artist*
Ruben Martinez
*Digital Artist Supervisor*
Zachary Foley
*Digital Artists*
Parker Paul
Justin Murphy
Steve Ilous
Todd Kale

**88–89 > CHANGE DIGITAL STUDIOS**
www.change.com

*Title*
I Hear Voices
*Flash Artist/Art Director*
Micah Laaker

*Video Director*
Jeff Martini
*Lead Programmer*
Alex Meyer
*Chief Creative Officer*
Nancy Duran
*Music Artist*
MF Doom
www.metalfacerecords.com/mfdoom
*Song*
I Hear Voices
*Record Company*
Metal Face Records
www.metalfacerecords.com

**90–91 > ONE INFINITY**
www.oneinfinity.com

*Title*
Thin Line Between Raw and Jiggy
*Flash Artist/Head Animator*
Eric Mauro
*Director*
Seth Fershko
*Writer*
Chris Martin
*Character Design and Art*
Cassady Benson
*Background Art*
Justin Chan
*Colorist*
Pat Lau
*Music Artist*
Dice Raw
www.diceraw.com
*Song*
Thin Line Between Raw and Jiggy
*Record Company*
MCA Records
www.mcarecords.com

**92–93 > SQUAREWAVE INTERACTIVE**
www.squarewaveinteractive.com

*Title*
Chemicals
www.the-control-group.com
*Flash Artists/Graphic Creative Directors*
Mike Wislocki
Andrew King
*Flash Lead Programmers*
Mike Wislocki
Andrew King
*Music Artist*
The Control Group
*Record Company*
Squarewave Music/Laturo Records
www.squarewaveinteractive.com

**94–95 > TIMEHEAD ENTERTAINMENT**
www.crashlander.com/

*Title*
Preschool ProtoCops: Mission 001:

Clash of the Toddlers
*Flash Artists*
James Hutchinson
Gareth Matthews
*Music Artist*
James Hutchinson

*Title*
Solar Wind
*Flash Artist*
James Hutchinson
*Music Artist*
James Hutchinson

**96–97 > UNTITLED_07**
www.untitled07.com

*Title*
Inertia
*Flash Artist*
Adam Boozer
*Music Artist*
Aerial
*Song*
Inertia

**98–103 > PIXELWURLD**
www.pixelwurld.com

*Title*
Never the Same
*Flash Artist*
Andres Moreta
*Flash Lead Programmer*
Miles Lightwood
*Producer*
Geri Lightwood
*Music Artist*
Supreme Beings of Leisure
www.sbleisure.com
*Song*
Never the Same
*Record Company*
Palm Pictures
www.palmpictures.com

*Title*
Strangelove Addiction
*Flash Artist*
Andres Moreta
*Flash Lead Programmer*
Miles Lightwood
*Producer*
Geri Lightwood
*Music Artist*
Supreme Beings of Leisure
www.sbleisure.com
*Song*
Strangelove Addiction
*Record Company*
Palm Pictures
www.palmpictures.com

*Title*
I Hate My Frickin' ISP
*Flash Artist*
Andres Moreta
*Flash Lead Programmer*
Miles Lightwood
*Producer*
Geri Lightwood
*Executive Producers*
Stuart S. Shapiro
Adam Spielberger
*Music Artist*
Todd Rundgren
*Song*
I Hate My Frickin' ISP
*Record Company*
Artemis Records
www.artemisrecords.com

**104–105 > PIRATENET**
www.piratenet.com

*Title*
Rolling Redknuckles
*Flash Artist*
Sam Egan
*Director*
Danielle Marleau
*Flash Lead Programmer*
Andrew Brandou
www.howdypardner.com
*Supervising Producer*
Andrew Brandou

*Title*
Dream Detective
*Flash Artist*
Sam Egan
*Artist*
Robert Williams
*Director*
Jordan Reichek
*Flash Lead Programmer*
Andrew Brandou
*Supervising Producer*
Andrew Brandou

*Title*
Bludd
*Director*
Danielle Marleau
*Flash Lead Programmer*
Andrew Brandou
*Supervising Producer*
Andrew Brandou

**106–111 > HEAVY**
www.heavy.com

*Title*
American Suck Countdown
*Designer*
Orion Tait

*Logo Design*
Kenneth Harris
*Creative Director*
Ryan Honey

*Title*
Sumozilla
*Director/Illustrator/Animator*
Geoff Carley
*Creative Director*
Ryan Honey
*Title*
Die Sushi Die
*Director/Illustrator/Animator*
Mike Judge
*Creative Director*
Ryan Honey

*Title*
Sumos Kill
*Director/Illustrator/Animator*
Mike Judge
*Creative Director*
Ryan Honey

*Title*
Munchyman and Fatty
*Director/Illustrator/Animator*
Geoff Carley
*Illustrator/Animator*
Jack Williams
*Illustrator/Animator*
Rich Kelly
*Creative Director*
David Carson

**112–113 > CALLIOPE STUDIOS**
www.calliopestudios.com

*Title*
People Spaces and Things
*Director*
Jean-David Boujnah
*Supervising Producer*
Peer Bazarini
*Flash Lead Programmer*
Jesse Jones

*Title*
Bureau Betak
*Director*
Jean-David Boujnah
*Supervising Producer*
Peer Bazarini

**114–117 > ICEBOX**
www.icebox.com

*Title*
Hard Drinkin' Lincoln
*Director*
Xeth Feinberg

*Flash Lead Programmer*
Xeth Feinberg
*Supervising Producer*
Mike Reiss

*Title*
Meet the Millers
*Directors*
Jerry Richardson
Wes Archer
*Flash Lead Programmers*
Remi Lortie
Sarbakan
*Supervising Producer*
David Zuckerman

*Title*
Mr. Wong
*Director*
Kyle Richardson
*Flash Lead Programmers*
Dusty Wakefield/Homer Reyes
*Supervising Producers*
Pam Brady
Kyle McCulloch

**118–121 > MAGRITTE'S COW**
www.magrittescow.com

*Title*
Against the Elements
*Interactive Flash Designers*
Daniel Szecket
Ronen Lasry
*Music Artist*
Confrontation Camp
www.slamjamz.com
www.rapstation.com
*Song*
Against the Elements
*Producers*
Walter Leaphart
Stuart S. Shapiro
Adam Speilberger
*Record Company*
Artemis Records
www.artemisrecords.com

*Title*
Maze Engine Game
*Interactive Flash Designers*
Daniel Szecket
Ronen Lasry

**128 >GOONLAND**
www.goonland.com

*Title*
Sweepin' Joe's
*Flash Artist/Programmer*
Mike Storey

> Italics indicates artists' statements.

> This book is dedicated to my mentor, Marcel Camus, who taught me the art of movement. An Orpheist, Marcel taught me that all objects carry a life force, thereby clarifying the effect and power of art and entertainment.

> stuart s. shapiro

> And to all the dot-com companies who crashed and burned while creating the Internet Revolution. May their unbridled energy be a source of inspiration to all of us who dare to jump off the cliff to fly to new heights.

> laurie dolphin & stuart s. shapiro